Ladybird  Readers

Racing with Scuderia Ferrari

Series Editor: Sorrel Pitts
Written by Sorrel Pitts

LADYBIRD BOOKS

UK | USA | Canada | Ireland | Australia
India | New Zealand | South Africa

Ladybird Books is part of the Penguin Random House group of companies
whose addresses can be found at global.penguinrandomhouse.com.
www.penguin.co.uk   www.puffin.co.uk   www.ladybird.co.uk

Penguin
Random House
UK

First published 2019
001

Published by arrangement with Franco Cosimo Panini Editore Spa, Modena, Italy www.paniniragazzi.it

Printed in China

A CIP catalogue record for this book is available from the British Library

ISBN: 978–0–241–36510–6

All correspondence to:
Ladybird Books
Penguin Random House Children's
80 Strand, London WC2R 0RL

Racing with
Scuderia Ferrari

Contents

Picture words

team

racetrack

gas

tire

flag

pit stop

overtake
(to get in front of another car)

champagne

trophy

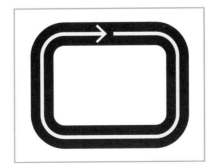

lap
(when a car goes once
around a track)

A Grand Prix race

A Grand Prix race is usually 190 miles long, and it takes about two hours to drive. Those two hours are very exciting!

Before the race

A lot of work happens before a Grand Prix. Six days before the race, Ferrari brings its team to the racetrack.

The Scuderia Ferrari team in 1965

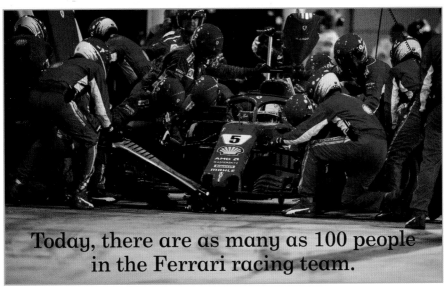

Today, there are as many as 100 people in the Ferrari racing team.

When the drivers and engineers arrive, they go to look at the racetrack. Most drivers have driven on it many times before, but they still need to look at it, because there may be changes.

The racing cars arrive in big Ferrari trucks.

Before a race, the team and the drivers study the racetrack very carefully. They walk around it first, and sometimes the drivers ride bicycles around it, too!

Felipe Massa riding a bicycle
around a racetrack

Practice

On the Friday before the race, each team has two lots of practice time before the first qualifying lap. There is another hour of practice on the Saturday before the second qualifying lap.

Ferrari's Sebastian Vettel practicing at the Abu Dhabi Grand Prix in 2017

The practice is used to get information. It tells the team how much gas, and which tires, their car needs.

The Ferrari team looking at information from a practice

If there is a lot of stopping and starting in the race, then the car needs more gas. But a lot of gas makes the car heavy.

The team looking at Sebastian Vettel's car

Qualifying

The qualifying laps decide each driver's starting place in Sunday's Grand Prix. The fastest driver starts at the front.

A qualifying lap

The driver must be careful
in qualifying. If the car hits
something or leaves the racetrack,
it cannot start again!

All the drivers want to start first in Sunday's big race, because it is often very difficult to overtake after the first corner.

Kimi Räikkönen overtaking
another car

Driving around corners

In the qualifying lap, it is very important to drive around the corners as fast as possible.
All the drivers practice the corners in the qualifying laps.

Ferrari's Kimi Räikkönen
driving around a corner

Starting places

At the end of Saturday's qualifying laps, the starting places are decided. The Ferrari team uses the qualifying information to think about changes to the car for Sunday—the day of the big race!

A Ferrari engineer and Vettel talking before a race

Thirty minutes before Sunday's Grand Prix begins, the cars are driven to their starting places. When a green light turns on, all the drivers do one lap of the racetrack.

Then, the cars go back to their starting places.

Cars at the start of a Grand Prix

The race!

Ten red lights come on. When they go off, the race starts!

How fast a driver starts the race is very important. This is the best time to overtake the other cars, so each driver tries to start as quickly as possible.

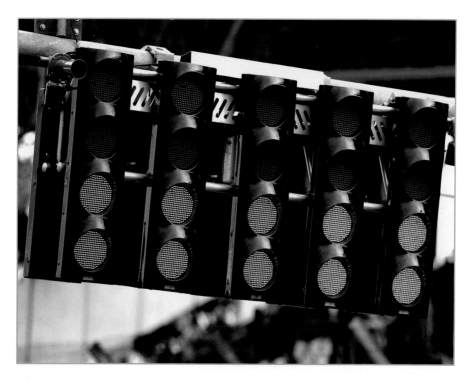

Starting lights at a Grand Prix

The first few seconds of a race are very exciting. The driver in front wants the other drivers to stay behind, so he drives across the track to try and stop them from overtaking.

Ferrari is in front!

Racetracks like Monaco or the Hungaroring are not very wide, so overtaking is very difficult. The driver who starts the race in front often wins.

The racetrack at Monaco

Some people say this is boring, but the drivers in front sometimes make mistakes!

The Hungaroring racetrack

Three things can help decide the winner of a race.

1. What each team has decided before the race starts: for example, how much gas they have put in the car, or which tires they choose.

Working on the car before a race

2. How quickly the racing driver starts the race.

A fast start for Ferrari!

3. How fast the car goes through the pit stops.

A car comes fast into a pit stop

Gas makes cars heavy and slow. Until 2010, cars started with very little gas and stopped at pit stops when they needed more.

Today, a car must start with enough gas to finish a whole race.

A car gets gas at a pit stop.

Pit stops

Cars still use pit stops for other things, like changing tires. There are usually one to three stops in a race.

The car must stop, change tires, and start again, in two or three seconds.

Changing tires at a pit stop

Other things can happen in the pit stop. Changes are sometimes made to a car's body.

This team is changing the tires of a car.

Winning a Grand Prix

The first driver to drive under the flag is the winner. After the race finishes, the car drives another lap, and the driver waves to the people watching.

GULF AIR

Ferrari's Sebastian Vettel wins the
Bahrain Grand Prix in 2018.

The happy driver gets the race trophy and throws champagne on the team and the other drivers.

Sadly, only one driver can win a Grand Prix. But all the people in the Scuderia Ferrari team feel like winners when their car comes first!

Ferrari's Michael Schumacher
with the race trophy

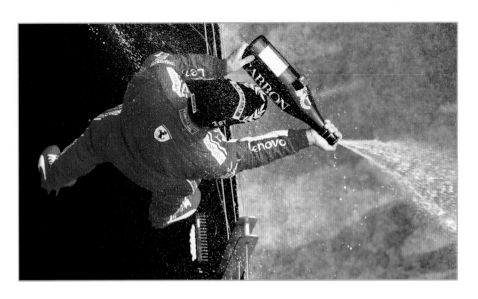

Sebastian Vettel with his team

Scuderia Ferrari drivers

Scuderia Ferrari is one of the best racing teams in the world. It has driven in Grand Prix races since 1950.

Here are some of its famous drivers.

Michael Schumacher is one of the most famous Ferrari racing drivers. He won five World Championships for Ferrari in 2000, 2001, 2002, 2003, and 2004.

Niki Lauda drove for Ferrari in the 1970s and won many races.

Jody Scheckter and Gilles Villeneuve came first and second in the 1979 World Championship.

Kimi Räikkönen won the World Driver's Championship for Ferrari in 2007.

Sebastian Vettel has won four World Championships and more than 50 Grand Prix races.

Activities

The key below describes the skills practiced in each activity.

🖊 Spelling and writing

📖 Reading

💬 Speaking

❓ Critical thinking

✴ Preparation for the Cambridge Young Learners exams

1 Find the words.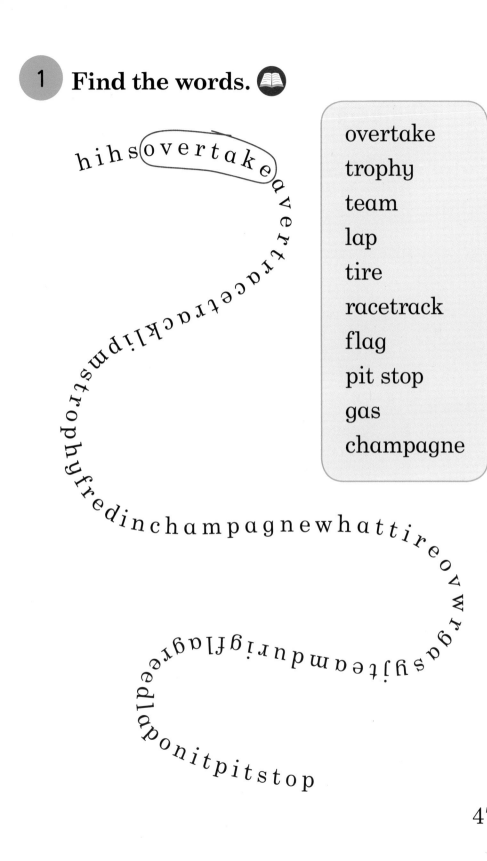

hihs overtake avertracetrackjipmstrophyfredinchampagnewhattireovwrgasyjteamdurigflagreedlaponitpitstop

overtake

trophy

team

lap

tire

racetrack

flag

pit stop

gas

champagne

2 Look and read. Write *yes* or *no*.

1  This is a racetrack.　　yes

2  This is a team. ....

3  This is a pit stop. ....

4  This is a trophy. ....

5  These are flags. ....

3 Read the questions. Write answers using the words in the box.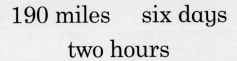

> 190 miles   six days
> two hours

1 How long is a Grand Prix race?

A Grand Prix race is usually 190 miles long.

2 How long does it take to drive a Grand Prix race?

3 When does Ferrari bring its team to the racetrack?

4 Match the two parts of the sentences. 📖

1 When the drivers and engineers arrive,

2 Most drivers have driven on it many times before,

3 Before a race, the team

4 They walk around it first,

5 On the Friday before the race,

a but they still need to look at it.

b and sometimes the drivers ride bicycles around it, too!

c each team has two lots of practice time.

d and the drivers study the racetrack carefully.

e they go to look at the racetrack.

5 **Read the text. Choose the correct words and write them on the lines.**

---

1 flags	trophies	tires
2 champagne	gas	overtake
3 laps	pit stops	teams
4 engineer	race	racetrack

---

1 The practice is used to tell the team how much gas, and which _tires_ , their car needs.

2 If there is a lot of stopping and starting in the race, then the car needs more
_____ .

3 The qualifying _____ decide each driver's starting place in Sunday's Grand Prix.

4 If the car hits something or leaves the _____ , it cannot start again!

6 Talk to a friend about the days before the Grand Prix. Answer the questions. 🗨 ⭐

1
> When does the racing team arrive at the racetrack?

> The team arrives six days before the race.

2 What do the drivers and engineers do before the race?

3 What information do the drivers get from the practice laps?

4 Why are the qualifying laps important to the drivers?

7 Write *and, but, so,* or *because.*

1 All the drivers want to start first in Sunday's big race, ...because.... it is often very difficult to overtake after the first corner.

2 It is very important to drive around the corners as fast as possible, ...
all the drivers practice them.

3 The starting places are decided,
.... the team can still make changes.

4 Before Sunday's Grand Prix begins, a green light is turned on, ...
all the drivers do one lap.

8 Look at the letters. Write the words.

1 (t c r e k a r a c)
Six days before the race, Ferrari brings
its team to the racetrack.

2 (m e a t)
There are as many as 100 people in
the Ferrari racing ....

3 (p a l)
On the Friday before the race, each
team has two lots of practice time before
the first qualifying ....

4 (r t s i e)
The practice is used to tell the team
how much gas, and which ....,
their car needs.

9 **Circle the correct sentences.**

1 **a** It is important to drive around the corners as fast as possible.

  b It is important to drive around the corners faster than possible.

2 **a** After Saturday's qualifying laps, the starting places are decided.

  b After Saturday's qualifying laps, the starting places are deciding.

3 **a** The Ferrari team doesn't use the qualifying information to think about changes to the car.

  b The Ferrari team uses the qualifying information to think about changes to the car.

4 **a** When a green light turns on, all the drivers do one lap of the racetrack.

  b When a green light turns off, all the drivers do one lap of the racetrack.

10 Circle the correct words.

1 How **fast** / **faster** a driver starts the race is very important.

2 This is the **good** / **best** time to overtake the other cars.

3 Each driver tries to start as **quicker** / **quickly** as possible.

4 The first few seconds of a race are very **excited,** / **exciting,** as the driver in front wants the other drivers to stay behind.

5 Racetracks like Monaco are not very **wide,** / **wider,** so overtaking is very difficult.

6 Some people say this is **bored,** / **boring,** but the drivers in front sometimes make mistakes!

11 **Complete the sentences.**
Write a—d.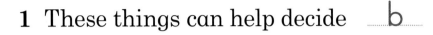

1 These things can help decide ......b......

2 What each team has decided ....

3 How quickly ....

4 How fast the car goes ....

---

a through the pit stops.

b the winner of a race.

c the racing driver starts the race.

d before the race starts.

12 **Work with a friend. Talk about the two pictures. How are they different?** 🗨

a

b

In picture a,
there are lots of cars.

In picture b,
there is only one car.

13 Read the text. Choose the correct words and write them next to 1—5.

started   needed   start   finish   stopped

Until 2010, cars ¹ .... started .... with

very little gas and ² .... at

pit stops when they ³ .... more.

Today, a car must ⁴ .... with

enough gas to ⁵ .... a whole race.

14 Read the sentences. Write
BR (before the race), *IR* (in the race)
or *AR* (after the race). 📖 ✏️ ❓

1 A driver does a
qualifying lap.   BR

2 A driver throws champagne
on the other drivers.   ....

3 A driver tries to overtake
other cars.   ....

4 A driver uses pit stops
to change tires.   ....

5 A driver waves to the
people watching.   ....

6 A driver goes to look
at the racetrack.   ....

15 Circle the correct pictures.

1 This is where you go to change tires.

 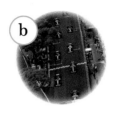 

2 This team has won the Grand Prix!

3 This part of the racetrack is straight.

 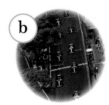 

4 He is overtaking.

16 Do the crossword.

Across

1 The winning driver gets a . . .
4 The first driver to drive under the . . . is the winner.
5 To get in front of another car.

Down

2 Where a driver goes for new tires.
3 Drivers throw . . . on the team when they win.

17 Talk to a friend about the different parts of a Grand Prix race. 💬

First, the cars go to their starting places. Then, . . .

Level 4

The Pied Piper of Hamelin

978-0-241-25378-6 ☐

The Wizard of Oz

978-0-241-25379-3 ☐

Sam and the Robots

978-0-241-25380-9 ☐

The Little Mermaid

978-0-241-29874-9 ☐

Peter and the Wolf

978-0-241-28434-6 ☐

Pinocchio

978-0-241-28430-8 ☐

Alice in Wonderland

978-0-241-28431-5 ☐

Heidi

978-0-241-28433-9 ☐

Aladdin

978-0-241-31606-1 ☐

Knights and Castles

978-0-241-28432-2 ☐

Under the Oceans

978-0-241-29888-6 ☐

Space

978-0-241-25381-6 ☐

A Fight with Underbite

978-0-241-29890-9 ☐

Sideswipe Loses his Head

978-0-241-29889-3 ☐

The Pony Games

978-0-241-31956-7 ☐

Forests

978-0-241-31958-1 ☐

Dangerous Journeys

978-0-241-29891-6 ☐

Racing with Scuderia Ferrari

978-0-241-36510-6 ☐

Now you're ready for Level 5!